COOKING COMICALLY
RECIPES SO EASY YOU'LL
ACTUALLY MAKE THEM

COOKING COMICALLY
RECIPES SO EASY YOU'LL ACTUALLY MAKE THEM

TYLER CAPPS

A PERIGEE BOOK

A PERIGEE BOOK
Published by the Penguin Group
Penguin Group (USA)
375 Hudson Street, New York, New York 10014, USA

USA | Canada | UK | Ireland | Australia | New Zealand | India | South Africa | China

Penguin Books Ltd., Registered Offices: 80 Strand, London WC2R 0RL, England
For more information about the Penguin Group, visit penguin.com.

COOKING COMICALLY

ISBN: 978-0-399-16404-0

First edition: October 2013

PRINTED IN THE UNITED STATES OF AMERICA

10 9 8 7 6 5 4 3 2

The recipes contained in this book are to be followed exactly as written. The publisher is not
responsible for your specific health or allergy needs that may require medical supervision. The publisher is
not responsible for any adverse reactions to the recipes contained in this book.

While the author has made every effort to provide accurate telephone numbers, Internet addresses, and
other contact information at the time of publication, neither the publisher nor the author assumes any responsibility
for errors, or for changes that occur after publication. Further, the publisher does not have any control over and
does not assume any responsibility for author or third-party websites or their content.

Most Perigee books are available at special quantity discounts for bulk purchases for sales promotions,
premiums, fund-raising, or educational use. Special books, or book excerpts, can also be created to fit specific needs.
For details, write: Special.Markets@us.penguingroup.com.

ALWAYS LEARNING   PEARSON

THIS SILLY BOOK IS
DEDICATED TO

JASON AND KAREN LAURITZEN

KAREN GAVE ME WORK WHEN I WAS DOWN
AND OUT AND ALONG WITH HER SON JASON
(ONE OF MY BEST AND OLDEST FRIENDS)
DONATED TO ME AN ENTIRE KITCHEN'S WORTH
OF SUPPLIES AND UTENSILS WHEN I MOVED
INTO MY CURRENT APARTMENT. MANY OF
WHICH WERE USED IN THE CREATION OF THIS
BOOK AND IN MY OWN EFFORTS TO LEARN TO
COOK.

THEIR KINDNESS AND FRIENDSHIP WILL NEVER
BE FORGOTTEN.

CONTENTS

Appetizers and Sides
PREFOOD FOOD AND FOOD TO
GO WITH YOUR OTHER FOOD

1

Breakfast
EATING: NOW AVAILABLE
BEFORE NOON

40

Lunch and Dinner
THE REAL MEAT AND POTATOES
OF THE BOOK, BUT NOT
ACTUALLY... WELL, SOME OF
THE TIME

70

Desserts
ABANDON ALL HOPE
(OF SWIMMING SHIRTLESS)
YE WHO ENTER HERE

154

Recipe Index and Metric Conversions
FOR THE COMMUNISTS

186

Appetizers and Sides

2

JALAPEÑO POPPERS

DIFFICULTY

READING THIS RECIPE IS ALMOST HARDER THAN MAKING IT

MAKES: 8

GET OUT ALL THE SHIT YOU NEED

HAVE YOUR JALAPEÑOS?

HALVE YOUR JALAPEÑOS.

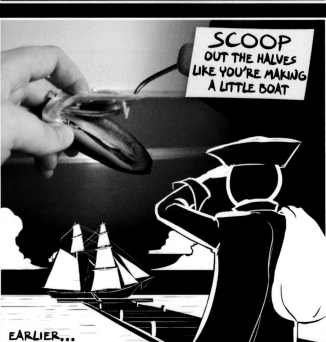

SCOOP OUT THE HALVES LIKE YOU'RE MAKING A LITTLE BOAT

EARLIER...

PACK THAT LITTLE BOAT FULL OF SWEET CREAMY CHEESE

SECURE THE CHEESE YOU DOGS!

4

Full Shopping list

REQUIRED:
JALAPEÑOS
BACON
CREAM CHEESE

OPTIONAL:
WIRE COOKING RACK

NOTES

- I DEFINITELY RECOMMEND USING THE WIRE RACK IF YOU'VE GOT ONE. IT CUTS WAY DOWN ON CLEAN UP.

- IF YOU CAN'T GET THE BACON TO STAY WRAPPED, USE A TOOTHPICK. I HAVEN'T HAD THIS PROBLEM THOUGH.

- A REGULAR SPOON SHOULD WORK FINE FOR SCOOPING THE JALAPEÑOS. JUST BE SURE YOU GET ALL THE SEEDS UNLESS YOU LIKE IT HOT.

7

DEM WEDGES

DIFFICULTY

YOU COULD ALMOST BE ASLEEP AND DO THIS

SERVES: 2ISH

AND OUT COME THE GROCERIES

RED POTATOES, OLIVE OIL, PARMESAN CHEESE, CAYENNE, OREGANO, GARLIC POWDER, ONION POWDER, BASIL, SALT AND PEPPER.

RINSE OFF YOUR POTATOES

DASH

~1 TBSP PARMESAN

1/2 TSP SALT

1/4 TSP BASIL

ADD

SHAKE IT

9

SLICE UP THEM POTATOES

ADD A DRIZZLE OF OLIVE OIL

~1 1/2 TBSP

TOSS TO COAT

ADD THE SEASONING

TOSS AGAIN

TO THE OVEN

350 F 45-55 MINUTES

AND WE'RE DONE

Full Shopping list

RED POTATOES (6)
PARMESAN (1 1/2TBSP)
OLIVE OIL (DRIZZLE)
OREGANO (DASH)
BASIL (1/4TSP)
CAYENNE (DASH)
SALT (1 1/2 TSP)
PEPPER (DASH)
GARLIC POWDER (DASH)
ONION POWDER (DASH)

Notes

- Serve with condiment of choice. I use ketcup myself.

- No, I don't actually want to punch you if you pronounce things differently.

- Other types of potatoes work just fine. Red is just a personal preference.

- Feel free to mix up the seasoning with whatever you think would be good.

Cheese in a Snuggie

SERVES: 4

DIFFICULTY

EASY AS LOOKING SILLY IN A SNUGGIE

PREPARE TO PREPARE FOODS

MOZZARELLA, PIZZA DOUGH, BASIL, ONION POWDER, GARLIC POWDER, TUMERIC, SALT, PEPPER, OREGANO, BUTTER AND MARINARA SAUCE

CUT THE CHEESE (FART JOKES LOL)

AND GET OUT YOUR DOUGH

1/2 POUND

UNROLL THE DOUGH AND PLACE CHEESE LIKE SO

PACK IT UP NICE

SEAL WELL

REPEAT

13

AND ENJOY

BAKE @350°F 10-15 MINUTES

FULL SHOPPING LIST

MOZZARELLA (1/2 LB)
PIZZA DOUGH (1 CAN)
GARLIC POWDER (1 TSP)
OREGANO (DASH)
SALT (DASH)
PEPPER (DASH)
TUMERIC (1/4 TSP)
BASIL (1/4 TSP)
ONION POWDER (1/4 TSP)
BUTTER (2 TBSP)
MARINARA SAUCE

NOTES

- IT'S BASICALLY A STUFFED CRUST PIZZA MINUS THE PIZZA. IF YOU THINK THAT'S A BAD THING, SOMETHING MIGHT BE WRONG WITH YOU.

- SERIOUSLY SEAL THE CHEESE IN AS BEST YOU CAN. OTHERWISE IT'LL JUST BE COOKED DOUGH SWIMMING IN HOT CHEESE. WHICH IS STILL AMAZING, BUT HARDER TO EAT WITH DIGNITY.

- GET IT? I'LL STOP THE WORLD AND MELT WITH YOU? ANYONE?

15

THE ARTICHOKE DIP

DIFFICULTY

COOK MUST BE CAN-OPENER CERTIFIED

SERVES: 6

RUSTLE UP SOME GROCERIES

16oz CANS

ARTICHOKE HEARTS, PARMESAN CHEESE, MAYO, GARLIC POWDER, AND SALT

OPEN ARTICHOKES AND DRAIN

SQUEEZE REMAINING WATER FROM ARTICHOKE HEARTS BEFORE CHOPPING

YOU CAN BUY THEM PRE-CUT BUT IT'S MORE EXPENSIVE...

THFFBBT

1 CUP

2 TSP

1/2 TSP

1 CUP

MIX

NOW TAKE IT TO A PARTY AND TIME HOW LONG IT LASTS...

Full Shopping List

ARTICHOKE HEARTS
(2 16oz CANS)

MAYO (1 CUP)

PARMESAN (1 CUP)

GARLIC POWDER (2TSP)

SALT (1/2TSP)

Notes

- THIS IS ESPECIALLY GOOD FOR GET-TOGETHERS. I'VE HONESTLY NEVER SEEN IT LAST MORE THAN 20 MINUTES.

- REPLACING SOME OF THE ARTICHOKE WITH SPINACH WORKS WELL TOO.

- IF YOU'D LIKE TO BUY FRESH PARMESAN AND GRIND UP A CUP'S WORTH, PLEASE DO.

B Corny Dread

Difficulty

YOU ARE TAKING YOUR LIFE INTO YOUR OWN HANDS.

SERVES: 8

RECIPE BY JILLIAN SAPP-MOODY

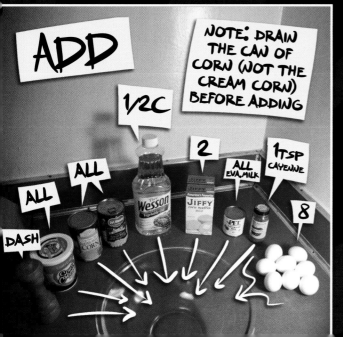

IF STILL ALIVE...
ENJOY

Full Shopping List

CORN MUFFIN MIX
(2 8.5oz PACKAGES)
SOUR CREAM (16oz)
EVAPORATED MILK (5oz CAN)
EGGS (8)
CAYENNE (1tsp)
VEGETABLE OIL (1/2CUP)
CORN (1 16oz CAN)
CREAM CORN (1 16oz CAN)

Notes

-YEP. ALL YOU DO IS PUT IT ALL IN A BOWL, MIX AND BAKE. THAT'S IT. AND SIMPLE AS IT IS IT'S STILL SOME OF THE BEST CORNBREAD I'VE FOUND.

- THIS'LL PRETTY MUCH FEED AN ARMY, YOU MIGHT THINK ABOUT HALVING THE RECIPE.

-THANKS, JILLIAN.

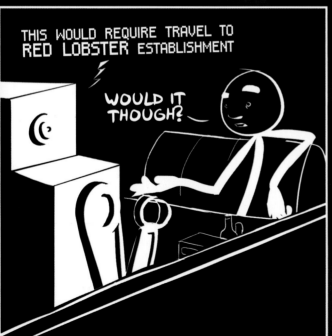

CHEDDAR-BOSS BISCUITS

DIFFICULTY

LITERALLY EASIER THAN GOING THERE AND HAVING THEM MADE FOR YOU.

SERVES: 4

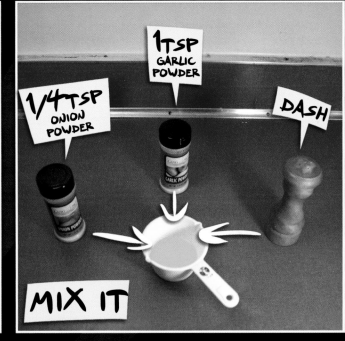

Full Shopping List

Butter (1/2 cup)
Baking mix (3 cups)
Cheddar cheese (1 cup)
Garlic powder (1 tsp)
Onion powder (1/4 tsp)
Salt (dash)

Notes

- Technically I think the garlic butter is supposed to have some parsley in it as well, but I don't like parsley so whatever.

- Flamethrower not a recommended kitchen utensil.

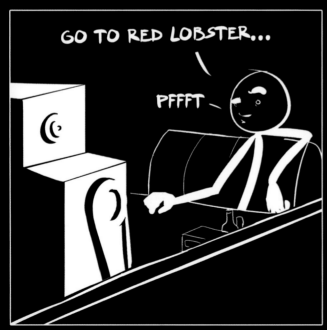

STEEZYMAC

MAC & CHEESE WITH STYLE AND EASE

DIFFICULTY

SLIGHTLY LESS EASY MAC

SERVES: 4

GET THE BAND BACK TOGETHER

NOODLES, CHEESE (I'M USING HAVARTI, CHEDDAR AND PARMESAN), EGGS, BUTTER, EVAPORATED MILK, HOT SAUCE, SALT AND PEPPER

GET NOODLES BOILING PRONTO

1 1/4 c

RUN YOUR CHEESE BY A SHREDDER

10/10 WOULD SHRED

DASH

1 TSP HOT SAUCE

ALL EV. MILK

2

ADD + MIX

STRAIN YOUR NOODLES

IN GOES 3TBSP OF BUTTER

STIR UNTIL MELTED

ADD EGG MIXTURE

AND CHEESE

STIR ON LOW HEAT UNTIL SMOOTH

SERVE

Full Shopping List

NOODLES (~1/2 LB)
EGGS (2)
CHEESE(S) OF CHOICE (1 1/4 CUPS)
EVAPORATED MILK (1 6 OZ CAN)
HOT SAUCE (1 TSP)
BUTTER (3 TBSP)
SALT (DASH)
PEPPER (DASH)

Notes

- I USED A COMBINATION OF HAVARTI, PARMESAN AND CHEDDAR CHEESES, BUT YOU CAN USE WHATEVER YOU LIKE. IT'S ALL VERY INTERCHANGABLE.

- I ALSO GRATED A LITTLE EXTRA PARMESAN ON TOP. TOASTED BREADCRUMBS ARE ALSO A GOOD IDEA.

- I'LL BET YOU DIDN'T KNOW THE SHREDDER WAS A CHEESE CRITIC.

35

MASH TATOES

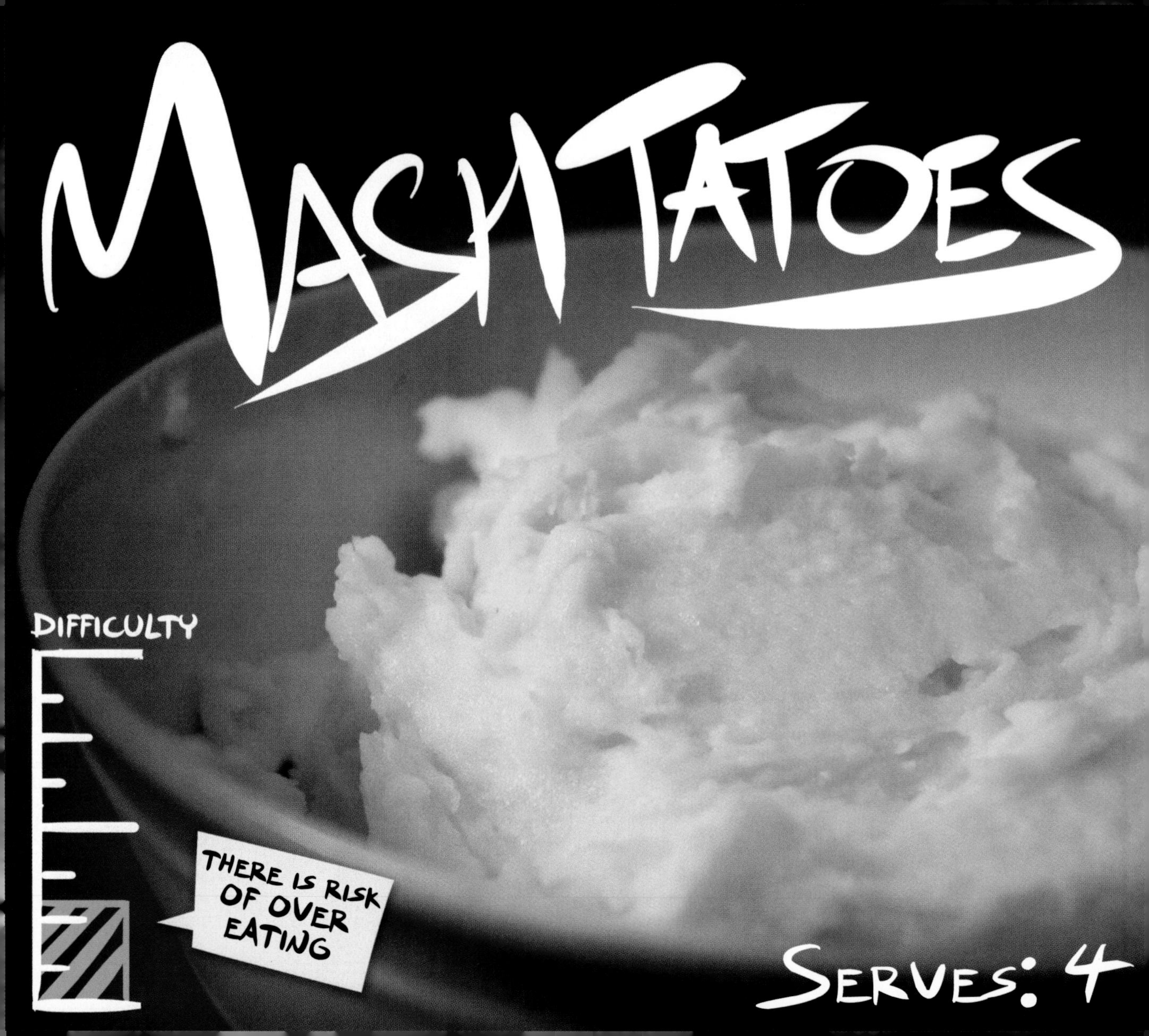

SALT AND PEPPER TO TASTE

AND ENJOY

Full Shopping List

GOLDEN POTATOES (5-6)
HEAVY CREAM (1/2 CUP)
BUTTER (1 STICK)
GARLIC (3 CLOVES)
PARMESAN (1/4 CUP)
SALT (DASH)
PEPPER (DASH)
POTATO MASHER

Notes

- I SHOULD PROBABLY APOLOGIZE TO NON-GAME OF THRONES READERS AND/OR WATCHERS. THAT WAS A LOT OF REFERENCES.

- WHEN YOU'RE MINCING THE GARLIC, THE FINER YOU CAN GET IT THE BETTER. OR USE A GARLIC PRESS IF YOU'VE GOT ONE.

- IF YOU WERE TO MAKE A STEW THOUGH... POTATOES ARE HIGHLY RECOMMENDED.

BREAKFAST

SEXY PANCAKES

DIFFICULTY

BRINGING SEXY
BACK TAKES A
LITTLE DOIN'

SERVES: 2

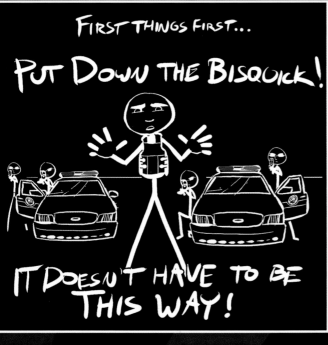

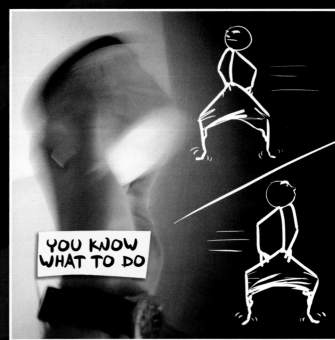

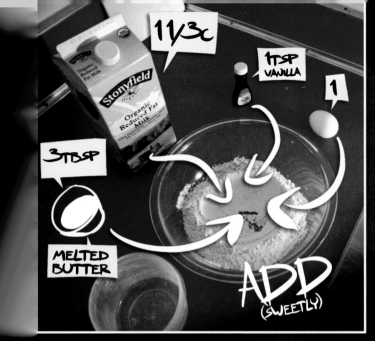

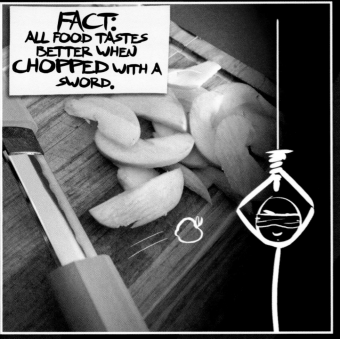

45

SYRUP!

NUTS!

WHIPPED CREAM!

SERVE HOT

PREFERABLY TO A PRETTY LADY/DUDE

Full Shopping List

FLOUR (1 1/2 CUPS)
BAKING POWDER (3 1/2 CUPS)
SUGAR (1 TBSP)
MILK (1 1/3 CUP)
EGG (1)
BUTTER (3 TBSP)
CINNAMON (1 TSP)
VANILLA EXTRACT
GRANNY SMITH APPLE (1)
PECANS
SYRUP OF CHOICE

Notes

- I'M SURE SOME WILL INSIST THAT YOU SIFT YOUR FLOUR AND OTHER DRY INGREDIENTS TOGETHER INTO THE BOWL. I'VE DONE THIS TOO AND THE DIFFERENCE WAS NOMINAL. BUT, IF YOU WANT TO AND YOU DON'T HAVE A SIFTER (I DIDN'T), A SPLATTER GUARD FOR A SKILLET WILL WORK..

- R.I.P. MR. WHITE. YOUR SEXINESS IS MISSED.

47

THE MACGUFFIN MUFFINS

DIFFICULTY

COMING TO THE CONCLUSION THAT NAZIS ARE BAD

SERVES: 4

RETRIEVE THE NECESSARY ITEMS

EGGS, BACON, CHEESE (CHEDDAR, MOZZARELLA, PEPPER JACK), CANNED BISCUITS (NOT THE FLAKY KIND), CAYENNE, ONION POWDER, GARLIC POWDER, SALT AND PEPPER

GET THAT BACON BAKIN' STRAIGHT AWAY

~30 MINUTES @ 400 F

THEY SEE ME ROLLIN' (BISCUITS)

THEY HATIN'

ADD DOUGH TO MUFFIN PAN AND REPEAT

CRACK

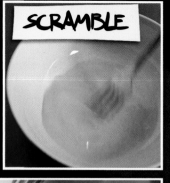

SCRAMBLE

ADD

1 EGG PER MUFFIN

ONION

CAYENNE

GARLIC

DASH

BACON IS DONE

SEEMS A BIT EXCESSIVE...

BACON? EXCESSIVE?

YOU BRING SHAME UPON YOURSELF AND THIS KITCHEN

GET OUT.

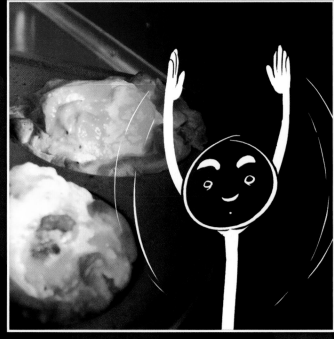

Full Shopping list

Eggs (6)
Canned biscuits (16oz)
Bacon (1 pack)
Cheese (Cheddar,
Mozzerella, Pepper
Jack)
Cayenne (dash)
Onion powder (dash)
Garlic powder (dash)
Salt (dash)
Pepper (dash)

Notes

—Again, this is a good basic template. Go nuts with it. Add fresh chopped onion, garlic, green peppers, different spices, cheeses, what have you.

— It doesn't matter how you cook your bacon, I just prefer to bake mine because it's cleaner.

— A MacGuffin is "a plot device in the form of some goal, desired object, or other motivator that the protagonist (and sometimes the antagonist) is willing to do and sacrifice almost anything to pursue."

MAPLE BACON

OR THE MEANING OF LIFE

DIFFICULTY

ABOUT AS HARD AS PREHEATING AN OVEN

SERVES: 2

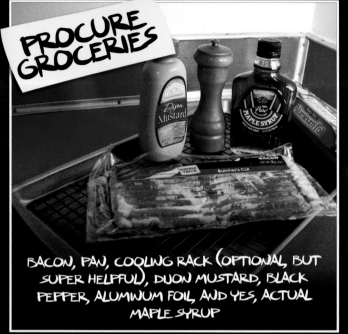

PROCURE GROCERIES

BACON, PAN, COOLING RACK (OPTIONAL, BUT SUPER HELPFUL), DIJON MUSTARD, BLACK PEPPER, ALUMINUM FOIL, AND YES, ACTUAL MAPLE SYRUP

TO THE OVEN FOR ~20 MINUTES @ 425F OR UNTIL 3/4 DONE

AS YOU LIKE

1 TSP

1/4 C

MIX IT UP

DAB OFF EXCESS GREASE

AND SLATHER GENEROUSLY

Full Shopping List

MAPLE SYRUP (1/4c)
DIJON MUSTARD (1TSP)
BLACK PEPPER (DASH)
BACON (1 PACK)
ALUMINUM FOIL
A BASTING BRUSH
IS NICE, BUT NOT
REQUIRED

Notes

- THE THICKNESS OF YOUR BACON WILL ALTER YOUR OVEN TEMPERATURE AND COOK TIMES. THIN BACON SHOULD BE ON 400 F FOR A SHORTER TIME.

- YES, ACTUAL MAPLE SYRUP THIS TIME. I HAVEN'T TRIED IT WITH ANYTHING ELSE YET SO I CAN'T SPEAK TO WHETHER OR NOT IT WOULD REALLY WORK WITH THE CHEAPER SYRUPS.

- I WOULD HIGHLY RECOMMEND USING A COOLING RACK. IT MAKES THINGS A LOT EASIER. AND I'M PARTIAL TO STRAIGHT BACON.

THE PERFECT SCRAMBLED EGG

DIFFICULTY

REQUIRES A LITTLE TIMING

SERVES: 2

GROCERIES. ON THE COUNTER.

EGGS, BUTTER, MILK, SALT

ONE-HANDED EGG CRACK **GRIP**

CRACK

SPREAD

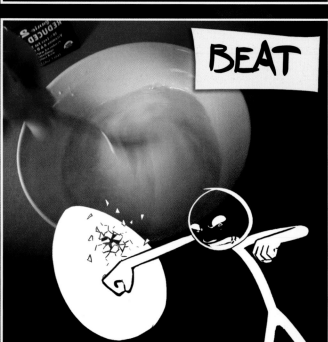

BEAT

ADD MILK (ABOUT 1 TBSP PER EGG) AND WHISK TOGETHER

Full Shopping list

MILK (4 TBSP)
EGGS (4)
BUTTER
(1/2 TBSP)
SALT
(OPTIONAL)

GUMPTION
(REQUIRED)

Notes

- IT MAY TAKE A COUPLE TRIES TO GET A FEEL FOR THE TIMING OF WHEN TO REMOVE THE EGGS, DON'T LET THAT DISCOURAGE YOU.

- I ALWAYS GUESSTIMATE THE MILK. IT'S NOT THAT BIG A DEAL.

- FEEL FREE TO THROW IN SOME CHEESE AND/OR SALT ONCE YOU'VE GOT THE BURNER ON HIGH.

- DON'T GO AROUND PUNCHING EGGS ALL WILLY-NILLY.

Oatmeal Pancakes

w/ raisins & brown sugar

DIFFICULTY

EASY AS NOT COMPROMISING

SERVES: 4

HUNT & GATHER
(BARGAINS) (FOODS)

BUTTERMILK, BROWN SUGAR, BAKING POWDER, BAKING SODA, SUGAR, EGG, ALL-PURPOSE FLOUR, OATS, OIL, VANILLA, RAISINS, SALT

3/4c BUTTERMILK

2TBSP VEG OIL

1TSP VANILLA

1

MIX UP WET INGREDIENTS

AND ADD THE REST

1TSP BAKING POWDER

1/2c OATS

1TBSP SUGAR

1/2c FLOUR

1TBSP B.SUGAR

1/2TSP BAKING SODA

RAISINS

1/2TSP SALT

STEER IT UP

JUST UNTIL COMBINED

SCOOP BATTER ONTO LIGHTLY OILED, PREHEATED SKILLET AND COOK AS NORMAL

SMELLS LIKE PURE UNADULTERATED BREAKFAST

CONSUME WITH A BIT OF SYRUP

Full Shopping List

BUTTERMILK (3/4 CUP)
BROWN SUGAR (1 TBSP)
BAKING POWDER (1 TSP)
BAKING SODA (1/2 TSP)
SUGAR (1 TBSP)
EGG (1)
ALL-PURPOSE FLOUR (1/2 CUP)
OATS (1/2 CUP)
OIL (2 TBSP)
VANILLA (1 TSP)
RAISINS (YOUR CHOICE)
SALT (1/2 TSP)

Notes

- SERIOUSLY, THE NUMBER ONE CULPRIT OF TOUGH PANCAKES IS OVERMIXING. SOME PEOPLE EVEN SAY TO ONLY MIX THE BATTER WITH TEN STROKES AND LEAVE IT NO MATTER WHAT.

- I ALMOST FEEL LIKE YOU COULD DITCH THE SYRUP AND DUNK THE PANCAKES IN MILK AS YOU GO INSTEAD...

BACON, EGG & CHEESE
CLASSY AS FUCK EDITION

DIFFICULTY

IT'S A SANDWICH FOR FUCK'S SAKE

SERVES: 4

STEP ONE

GO TO YOUTUBE.

SEARCH "MILES DAVIS" AND CLICK THE FIRST LINK THAT COMES UP.

CROISSANT, EGGS, TOMATO, CHEESE, MUSTARD, SYRUP, BACON, SALT/PEPPER, MILK, CHIPOTLE POWDER, CHIPOTLE W ADOBO SAUCE, LIME JUICE, CUMIN, GARLIC POWDER, MAYO

GET THE BACON STARTED

MAPLE BACON

OR THE MEANING OF LIFE

SEE PAGE 53

MIX UP THE AIOLI

3 TBSP MAYO

1/2 TSP CHIPOTLE AND GARLIC

DASH

1 TSP ADOBO (SAUCE ONLY)

2 TSP LIME JUICE

DASH CUMIN

SLICE

AND AGAIN

THROW YOUR TOMATOES W THE PAN WITH A DASH OF PEPPER FOR A MINUTE

I DO SAY, THAT SMELLS CLASSY AS FUCK

SCRAMBLE 3 EGGS ...PERFECTLY

SEE PAGE 58

ASSEMBLE

ENJOY

...CLASSILY.

Full Shopping list

CROISSANT (1)
EGGS (4)
TOMATO
CHEESE
MUSTARD (1 TSP)
SYRUP (1/4 CUP)
BACON
SALT/PEPPER (DASH)
MILK (4 TBSP)
CHIPOTLE POWDER (1/2 TSP)
CHIPOTLE W ADOBO SAUCE (1 TSP)
LIME JUICE (2 TSP)
CUMIN (DASH)
GARLIC POWDER (1/2 TSP)
MAYO (3 TBSP)

Notes

— THIS IS COMPLETELY OPEN TO CHANGES.
IT'S ALMOST MORE OF A RECOMMENDATION
THAN A RECIPE PROPER.

— DON'T LEAVE YOUR TOMATOES ON THE
PAN TOO LONG. YOU DON'T WANT THEM
SOGGY.

— BOWTIES ARE COOL.

LUNCH AND DINNER

LET'S FACE IT. THE KITCHEN HAS HAD AN IMAGE PROBLEM.

LESS SO NOW, BUT IN THE PAST

IT'S BEEN SEEN AS A PLACE FOR LADIES AND I CAN'T UNDERSTAND HOW THE HELL THAT EVER HAPPENED.

LOOK AT YOUR KITCHEN. IT HAS BEER, MEAT, KNIVES, SHARP STICKS, FIRE, RADIATION, CAFFEINE, SNACKAGE...

IT'S THE BEST ROOM IN YOUR HOUSE AND YOU'RE GOING TO LET IT BE MONOPOLIZED BY A SINGLE GENDER!?

NEGATIVE.

PULLED PORK
(OPERATION MAN-KITCHEN)

DIFFICULTY

WAITING WITH THE SMELL IS A MILD FORM OF TORTURE

SERVES: 6

LOCK & LOAD

PORK SHOULDER, ONION, BBQ SAUCE, CAYENNE, OREGANO, CLOVES, ALLSPICE, PAPRIKA, CUMIN, GARLIC POWDER, CHILI POWDER, SALT AND PEPPER (PINEAPPLE JUICE OPTIONAL)

BOOM
7 LBS OF BOSTON BUTT

BOSTON BUTT ISN'T ACTUALLY BUTT. IT'S SHOULDER

WRAP HALF UP FOR FREEZING

IT'S 4 PM

DO YOU KNOW WHERE YOUR BEER IS?

1/4 CUP OF BROWN SUGAR, 1 TSP OF PEPPER, GARLIC POWDER, PAPRIKA, CUMIN, CAYENNE, SALT AND OREGANO

THERE WAS A SEASONING

RUB *RUB*

2 WHOLE ONIONS GET CHOPPED AND POTTED

ADD 1 CUP OF WATER

AND A SHOT OF BEER

AND FINALLY A GOOD DUSTING OF CLOVES

COVER AND SET TO LOW FOR 8 HOURS

75

THAT SMELL... MY GOD

SOMEBODY GET ME A BEAR TO WRESTLE!

SHRED

TAKE THE PORK OUT, REMOVE FROM BONE AND SHRED USING TWO FORKS TO PULL ALL THE MEAT APART

CLEAN OUT THE SLOW COOKER AND ADD THE SHREDDED PORK BACK IN ALONG WITH YOUR FAVORITE BBQ SAUCE (HOWEVER MUCH YOU PREFER)

SET TO HIGH FOR ANOTHER 1-2 HOURS

DONE

AND JUST LIKE THAT YOU'VE GOT THE TASTIEST, JUICIEST PULLED PORK YOU CAN MAKE INSIDE A COMMON KITCHEN

Full Shopping list

PORK SHOULDER (3 1/2 LBS)
ONION (2)
BBQ SAUCE (~16 OZ)
CAYENNE (1 TSP)
OREGANO (1 TSP)
CLOVES (~2 TSP)
ALLSPICE (1 TSP)
PAPRIKA (1 TSP)
CUMIN (1 TSP)
GARLIC POWDER (1 TSP)
CHILI POWDER (1 TSP)
SALT AND PEPPER (1 TSP)
BROWN SUGAR (1/4 CUP)

Notes

-The onions are discarded, but their sacrifice was not in vain, I promise you.

- Choose a good sauce. If you have a BBQ joint you like, chances are they sell their sauce at the restaurant. That's a good place to start.

- Yes there is pineapple in the grocery photo. But I honestly couldn't taste a difference between using pineapple juice and using water, and water is cheaper.

SUPER
TERIYAKI BURGER II

SPECIAL CHAMPION EDITION

DIFFICULTY

PSSSSH

SERVES: 4

GROCERIES ASSEMBLE

GROUND BEEF, BUNS, BBQ SAUCE, PINEAPPLE SLICES, OLIVE OIL, ONION, LETTUCE, SOY SAUCE, TERIYAKI SAUCE, GARLIC POWDER, CAYENNE, MONTEREY JACK CHEESE

PREP YOUR KITCHEN

CLEAVE 1/4 OF YOUR ONION

WITH SCIENCE!

1 TBSP OF OLIVE OIL!

SMELLS

ONIONS!

OF

SAUTÉ!

TRIUMPH

SEE NEXT

1 TSP SOY

2 1/2 TBSP TERIYAKI

1 POUND GROUND BEEF

PROGRESSO BREAD CRUMBS

KIKKOMAN Soy Sauce

ALL-PURPOSE KIKKOMAN Teriyaki Marinade & Sauce

McCormick Garlic Powder

Ground Red Pepper

1/2 TSP GARLIC AND CAYENNE

ALL

NOW GET IN THERE AND MAKE MIKE ROWE PROUD

ADD BREADCRUMBS AS NEEDED. SHOULD BE JUST DRY ENOUGH TO FORM PATTIES.

FORM UP THEM PATTIES

HADOOKEN!

SPLAT

FREEZE UP WHAT YOU DON'T USE FOR LATER. (WHICH SHOULDN'T BE LONG AFTER YOU TASTE THE BURGER)

Nutrition Facts

SEE DIAGRAM OF OPTIMAL CONSTRUCTION AND PROCEED WITH CONSUMPTION

BUN
BBQ SAUCE
ONION
PINEAPPLE
CHEESE
BURGER
LETTUCE
BUN

FULL SHOPPING LIST

GROUND BEEF (1LB)
TERIYAKI SAUCE (2 1/2 TBSP)
SOY SAUCE (1 TSP)
GARLIC POWDER (1/2 TSP)
CAYENNE (1/2 TSP)
BREADCRUMBS (AS NEEDED)
HAMBURGER BUNS (1-4)
PINEAPPLE SLICES (1-4)
OLIVE OIL (1 TBSP)
EGGS (1)
YELLOW ONION (1)
LETTUCE
MONTEREY JACK CHEESE
BBQ SAUCE OF YOUR CHOICE
(I RECOMMEND A SWEET
TOMATO-BASED KIND)

NOTES

- WHILE THIS RECIPE IS FOR 4 BURGERS, I WAS ONLY COOKING FOR MYSELF THIS NIGHT. THUS, I ONLY COOKED 1 BURGER AND USED 1/4 THE ONION. FOR 4 BURGERS USE THE WHOLE ONION.

- IF YOU THINK IT NEEDS MORE TERIYAKI, ADD IT.

- I SUGGEST YOU SERVE IT WITH FRIES AND A BROWN ALE OF YOUR CHOICE.

BOLOGNESE FOR DAYS

DIFFICULTY

MUST BE ABLE TO OPERATE A POT

SERVES: 4

CONVENE GROCERIES

CRUSHED TOMATOES, WHOLE PLUM TOMATOES, BEEF, ONION, OREGANO, BASIL, GARLIC, SUGAR, OLIVE OIL, SALT AND PEPPER

DISSECT ONION AND GARLIC WITH EXTREME PREJUDICE

1/2

4 CLOVES

ADD OLIVE OIL AND GET YOUR SAUTE ON

MEANWHILE

2 TSP SUGAR

ALL

3 TSP OREGANO

ALL

3 TSP BASIL

1 TSP

ADD SAUTÉED VEGGIES AND A SHOT OF BEER

ALREADY SMELLS LIKE HEAVEN

BEEF

BROWN IT AND ADD TO THE POT

LET SIMMER ON LOW HEAT 1-3 HOURS

WHILE YOU WAIT...

EXPLORE YOUR ITALIAN HERITAGE

ENJOY

Full Shopping list

TOMATOES:
CRUSHED (28oz)
WHOLE PLUM (28oz)
ONION (1/2)
GARLIC (4 CLOVES)
BASIL (3TSP)
SUGAR (2TSP)
OREGANO (3TSP)
SALT (1TSP)
PEPPER (1TSP)
OLIVE OIL (~1 1/2TBSP)
GROUND BEEF (1/2LB)

Notes

- THIS IS MEANT TO BE A SUPER SIMPLE TEMPLATE FOR A RED SAUCE. IT'S HUGELY FLEXIBLE AND I'LL BE USING IT IN MANY MORE RECIPES TO COME.

- WHEN BROWNING THE BEEF AND ADDING IT TO THE POT ADD SOME OF THE GREASE AS WELL. TRUST ME, IT'S GOOD.

- DO NOT USE A CHAINSAW IN YOUR KITCHEN. UNLESS YOU'RE REMODELING. EVEN THEN REALLY... NOT THE BEST IDEA.

THAT'S MY JAMBALAYA

DIFFICULTY

THE OPPOSITE OF CALCULUS

SERVES: 4

MAKE A LIST CHECK IT TWICE

ANDOUILLE SAUSAGE, CHICKEN BREASTS, GREEN PEPPER, GARLIC, ONION, PARBOILED RICE, HOT SAUCE, CHICKEN STOCK, CAYENNE, TOMATO SAUCE, BASIL, CELERY, SALT AND PEPPER

CHOP

2 CLOVES GARLIC

1 1/2 CUPS ANDOUILLE

1/4 c ONION

1/4 c CELERY

1/4 c GREEN PEPPER

ALL TO THE PAN

SAUTÉ

DO WE REALLY NEED ANYTHING ELSE? I COULD JUST EAT THAT...

Full Shopping List

ANDOUILLE SAUSAGE (1 1/2 C)
CHICKEN BREAST (2)
GREEN PEPPER (1/4 C)
GARLIC (2 CLOVES)
ONION (1/4 C)
PARBOILD RICE (2 C)
HOT SAUCE (1 TBSP)
CHICKEN STOCK (2 C)
CAYENNE (2 TSP)
TOMATO SAUCE (2 C)
BASIL (1 TBSP)
CELERY (1/4 C)
SALT AND PEPPER (DASH)

Notes

- I FIND THE PARBOILED RICE IS ACTUALLY IMPORTANT. REGULAR RICE TAKES WAY TOO LONG TO BECOME SOFT IN THE MIX.

- THE ULTIMATE COLD WEATHER MEAL.

- THIS IS THE CREOLE VERSION OF JAMBALAYA, ALSO CHECK OUT THE CAJUN KIND.

THE CHICKENIEST CHICKEN SOUP

DIFFICULTY

ON PAR WITH SHOE-TYING

SERVES: 4

COLLECT YOUR FOODS

2 CANS CREAM OF CHICKEN, CHICKEN BREAST, CARROTS, MIXED VEGGIES, CELERY, POTATOES, OREGANO, CHICKEN BOUILLON CUBES, SALT AND PEPPER

CHOP

2 BONELESS SKINLESS CHICKEN BREASTS

5 MEDIUM POTATOES AND 1/2 CUP OF CELERY

AND 1/2 CUP OF CARROTS

ADD TO SLOW COOKER

WITH A DASH OF PEPPER

1/2 TSP SALT

AND 1/2 TSP GARLIC POWDER

ADD

1½ CANS +½ (Cream of CHICKEN, Cream of CHICKEN)

3 CUBES

COOK ON HIGH 5 HOURS

ADD MIXED VEGGIES

QUICK FROZEN FOR FRESHNESS
Mixed Vegetables
Grade A Fancy

NET WT. 16 OZ. (1 LB.) 454g

COOK 1 MORE HOUR

DONE

Full Shopping list

CREAM OF CHICKEN
(1½ 28oz CANS)
BONELESS SKINLESS CHICKEN
BREASTS (2)
CARROTS (½c)
MIXED VEGGIES (16oz)
CELERY (½c)
RED POTATOES (5)
OREGANO (½TSP)
CHICKEN BOUILLON CUBES (3)
SALT AND PEPPER (½TSP)

Notes

- THIS GOES EXTREMELY WELL WITH THE BREAD BOWLS ON PAGE 108.

- THERE REALLY ISN'T ANYTHING LIKE A GOOD HEARTY SOUP WHEN YOU'RE SICK. OR ANY OTHER TIME REALLY.

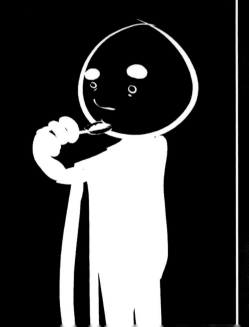

2AM CHILL

DIFFICULTY

THERE'S A WAIT INVOLVED

SERVES: 4

GROUND BEEF, GREEN PEPPER, GARLIC, ONION, SOUR CREAM, CHEDDAR, SALTINES, GREEN BEANS, TOMATO SAUCE, DICED TOMATOES, BROWN SUGAR, CORN, LIGHT RED KIDNEY BEANS

DID YOU BUY SOMETHING LIKE THIS?

COOL

NOW THROW THAT SHIT AWAY

WE DO IT LIVE!!

2 TBSP FLOUR

1 TSP BASIL

1 1/2 TBSP CHILI POWDER

1 TBSP CAYENNE

2 TSP SUGAR

1 TBSP ONION POWDER

2 TSP CUMIN

1 TBSP GARLIC POWDER

BROWN THAT BEEF

AND MEANWHILE...

CHOP

1/2

3-4 CLOVES

SAFTEY FIRST: "WE'RE FRAGILE CREATURES. IT TAKES LESS THAN A POUND OF PRESSURE TO CUT SKIN."
HUR HUR...

1/2

OPEN AND COMBINE THE CANS

BE SURE TO DRAIN THE BEANS AND CORN FIRST OR THEY'LL WATER DOWN YOUR MIX

STATUS CHECK: DOES YOUR STOVE LOOK ABOUT LIKE THIS?

GOOD

BEEF DONE?

DRAIN IT AND ADD TO THE POT. CLEAN YOUR SKILLET AND GET READY TO SAUTÉ SOME SHIT.

SAUTÉ VEGGIES

LIKE A BOSS

ADD THEM VEGGIES

ADD THAT SEXY SEASONING AND A COUPLE HEALTHY PINCHES OF BROWN SUGAR

AND A SHOT OF WHATEVER BEER YOU HAVE ON HAND

BRING YOUR MANLY CONCOCTION TO A BOIL. REDUCE HEAT AND SIMMER FOR AS MANY HOURS AS YOU'VE GOT.

STIR OCCASIONALLY

READY!

SWEET!

CRACKERS!

BABY!

CHEESE!

JESUS!

Full Shopping List

The Base:
TOMATO SAUCE (1 28OZ CAN)
TOMATO SAUCE (1 15OZ CAN)
DICED TOMATOES (1 15OZ CAN)
GREEN BELL PEPPER (1/2)
GARLIC (3-4 CLOVES)
ONION (1/2)
GROUND BEEF (1 1/2 LBS)
LIGHT RED KIDNEY BEANS (1-2 15OZ CANS)
GREEN BEANS (1 15OZ CAN)
CORN (1 15OZ CAN)
BROWN SUGAR (~1 1/2 TBSP)
COOKING OIL OF YOUR CHOICE (~2 TBSP)

The Seasoning:
ALL-PURPOSE FLOUR (2 TBSP)
SUGAR (2 TSP)
GARLIC POWDER (1 TBSP)
ONION POWDER (1 TBSP)
CAYENNE (1 TBSP)
CHILI POWDER (1.5 TBSP)
CUMIN (2 TSP)
BASIL (1 TSP)
PEPPER (1 TSP)

Recommended Toppings:
OYSTER CRACKERS/MINI SALTINES
SHREDDED SHARP CHEDDAR
SOUR CREAM

HOUSTON WE HAVE GROCERIES

BASIL, OREGANO, PIZZA DOUGH, OLIVE OIL, GREEN AND RED PEPPERS, ONION, GARLIC, MOZZARELLA, ITALIAN SAUSAGE, PEPPERONI, PARMESAN, COLBY/MONTEREY JACK CHEESE, MARINARA SAUCE

FOLLOWED BY CHEESE

BEGIN CONSTRUCTION WITH SAUSAGE

AND THEN SAUCE

SAUCE OVER CHEESE?!

THIS IS BLASPHEMY!

THIS IS MADNESS!

HATER

MADNESS?

THIS IS DEEP DISH

ONION, PEPPERONI, RED+GREEN PEPPERS, OREGANO (DASH), BASIL (DASH), GARLIC

COLBY AND MONTEREY JACK CHEESE, PARMESAN AND A DRIZZLE OF OLIVE OIL

BAKE 30-35 MINS @400F

AND VOILÁ

Full Shopping List

PIZZA DOUGH
OLIVE OIL (~1 1/2 TBSP)
BASIL (DASH)
OREGANO (DASH)
MOZZARELLA (ENOUGH TO
COVER PIZZA)
PARMESAN (UP TO YOU)
ONION (1/2)
PEPPERONI (UP TO YOU)
SAUSAGE (4-5 LINKS)
MONTEREY+COLBY CHEESE
(UP TO YOU)
MARINARA SAUCE (~16oz)
GREEN PEPPER (1/2)
RED PEPPER (1/2)

Notes

- If you've got a cast-iron skillet, use that instead.

- I find that most of the ingredients and amounts depend on your personal preference. Toppings/type of toppings especially. Go nuts.

- Yes, deep-dish pizza is commonly assembled in reverse of "standard" pizza.

- Thanks to Santos Loo for a delicious recipe.

FUCKING BREAD BOWLS
FROM SCRATCH

DIFFICULTY

YOU'RE GONNA SEE SOME SERIOUS SHIT

SERVES: 4

GET IT TOGETHER

ALL-PURPOSE FLOUR, DRY ACTIVE YEAST, EGG, CORNMEAL, COOKING OIL, SALT, WATER, HAND MIXER

1¼C WATER

ADD THAT YEAST TO WARM WATER. (JUST AS HOT AS YOUR FAUCET WILL GET)

ALL

LET IT DISSOLVE UNTIL IT LOOKS ABOUT LIKE THIS

10-15MINS

IN THE MEANTIME WE NEED TO TAKE AN EGG YOLK FROM HERE

AND MOVE IT OVER HERE

GET A PLASTIC BOTTLE

SQUEEZE AND PLACE GENTLY OVER THE TOP OF THE YOLK

BUT MR. COOKING GUY, HOW DO I SEPARATE THE YOLK FROM THE WHITES?

RELEASE

WHHAAAAT

WHITES TO THE FRIDGE FOR LATER

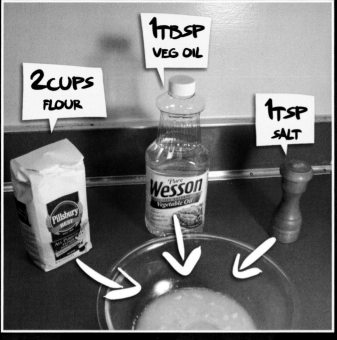

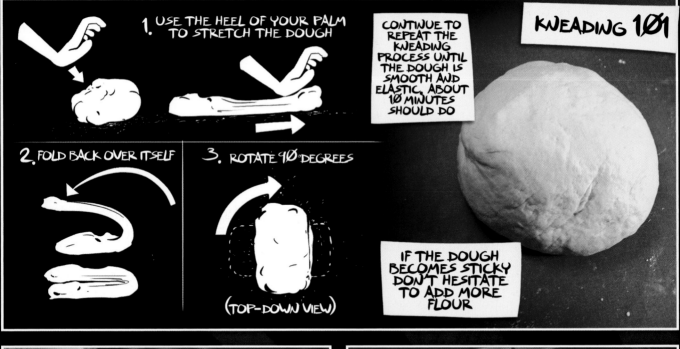

KNEADING 101

1. USE THE HEEL OF YOUR PALM TO STRETCH THE DOUGH

2. FOLD BACK OVER ITSELF

3. ROTATE 90 DEGREES

(TOP-DOWN VIEW)

CONTINUE TO REPEAT THE KNEADING PROCESS UNTIL THE DOUGH IS SMOOTH AND ELASTIC. ABOUT 10 MINUTES SHOULD DO

IF THE DOUGH BECOMES STICKY DON'T HESITATE TO ADD MORE FLOUR

DRIZZLE A LITTLE OIL INTO A LARGE BOWL. ADD IN YOUR DOUGH BALL AND SPIN IT AROUND TO COAT IT

COVER WITH A DAMP CLOTH OR PAPER TOWEL AND LEAVE IT IN A WARM (ROOMTEMP) PLACE FOR 40 MIN

GO AHEAD AND GREASE YOUR PAN (11"x17") AND SPRINKLE WITH WITH CORNMEAL

EMBIGGENED!
THE DOUGH HAS NOW RISEN AND ALMOST DOUBLED IN SIZE

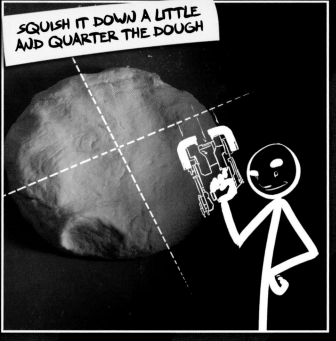

SQUISH IT DOWN A LITTLE AND QUARTER THE DOUGH

THESE WILL BECOME THE BOWLS SO GET THEM AS ROUND AS YOU CAN AND PLACE THEM ON THE BAKING SHEET

COVER AND LET RISE (SAME AS BEFORE) FOR ANOTHER 30 OR SO MINUTES

PREHEAT OVEN 400 F

WHILE THAT MAGIC IS GOING DOWN GET OUT THE EGGS WHITES AND MIX IN WATER

1/2 TBSP WATER

BRUSH THE SOON-TO-BE LOAVES WITH HALF OF THE EGG WHITES

BAKE 15 MINUTES

114

CUT!

REMOVE!

GO FORTH AND IMPRESS THE SHIT OUT OF SOMEONE

HOLLOW OUT FURTHER WITH A SPOON

LEAVE WALLS ~1/2 INCH THICK

Full Shopping list

DRY ACTIVE YEAST
(1/4 OZ PACK)
COOKING OIL (1 TBSP)
EGG (WHITES OF 1)
FLOUR (3 1/2 CUPS)
CORNMEAL (~1 TBSP)
SALT (1 TSP)
HAND MIXER

Notes

- This recipe is more resilient to fuck-ups than you might think. I made a giant mess the first time I tried it, but the bread turned out just about perfect. So don't stress.

- I highly recommend a tall bowl for mixing if you have one. My mixer flung dough everywhere.

- Be patient.

- A thick soup is best for the bowls like a nice chunky potato or french onion.

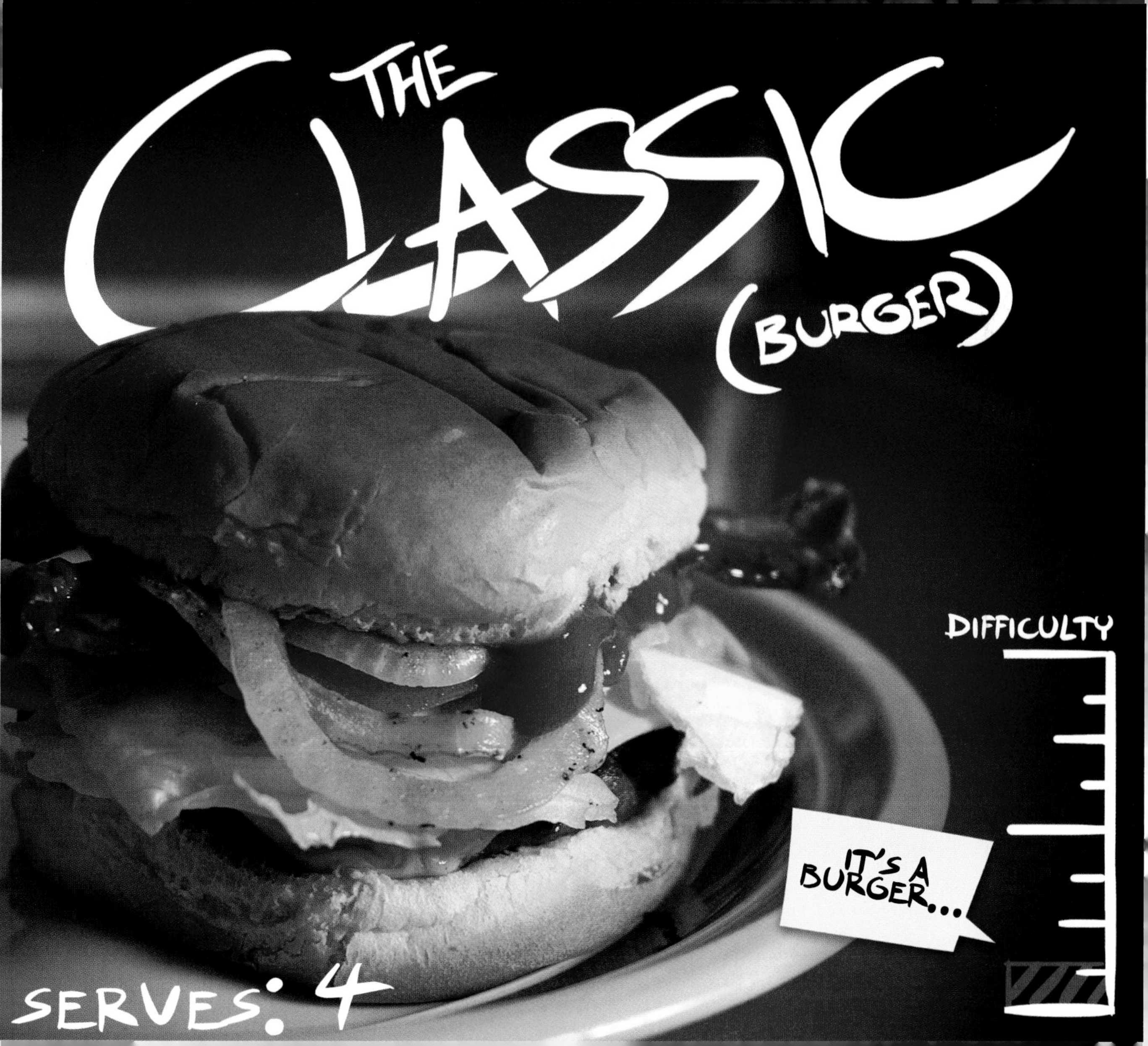
THE CLASSIC
(BURGER)
DIFFICULTY
IT'S A BURGER...
SERVES: 4

BREAK OUT THEM FOODS

GROUND BEEF, BREADCRUMBS,
BROWN SUGAR, CAYENNE,
ONION POWDER, GARLIC POWDER, PAPRIKA,
WORCESTERSHIRE SAUCE

RECOMMENDED TOPPINGS

KETCHUP, MUSTARD, BUNS, LETTUCE, ONIONS,
TOMATO, CHEESE, LEFTOVER BACON

DASH
GARLIC

DASH
ONION

1 TSP
B. SUGAR

DASH
CAYENNE

1 1/2 TSP
WORCESTERSHIRE

1/4 C
BREAD
CRUMBS

DASH
PAPRIKA

1

TO THE BOWL

PLAY WITH YOUR MEAT

ADD BREADCRUMBS
AS YOU DO TO
DRY IT OUT JUST
ENOUGH TO FORM
PATTIES

ONCE IT'S ALL MIXED FORM UP THEM PATTIES

FREEZE UP WHAT YOU DON'T WANT TO USE

COOK ON MEDIUM-LOW HEAT

OR THROW IT ON THE GRILL IF YOU'VE GOT ONE HANDY

HIT WITH ADDITIONAL WORCESTERSHIRE SAUCE WHILE COOKING

Full Shopping list

BUNS
KETCHUP
MUSTARD
CHEESE
LETTUCE
TOMATO
BACON
ONION

GROUND BEEF (1LB)
BREADCRUMBS
(AS NEEDED)
CAYENNE (DASH)
BROWN SUGAR (1TSP)
GARLIC POWDER (DASH)
ONION POWDER (DASH)
PAPRIKA (DASH)
WORCESTERSHIRE SAUCE
(1 1/2TSP)

NOTES

- THIS IS MY FAVORITE GO-TO BURGER FOR COOKOUTS.

- PLEASE, BY ALL MEANS, USE WHATEVER CHEESE YOU LIKE. I DON'T ACTUALLY THINK YOU'RE A FASCIST.

- ALSO USE WHATEVER TOPPINGS YOU LIKE. IT GOES WELL WITH JUST ABOUT EVERYTHING.

- POOR MEAT BOY...

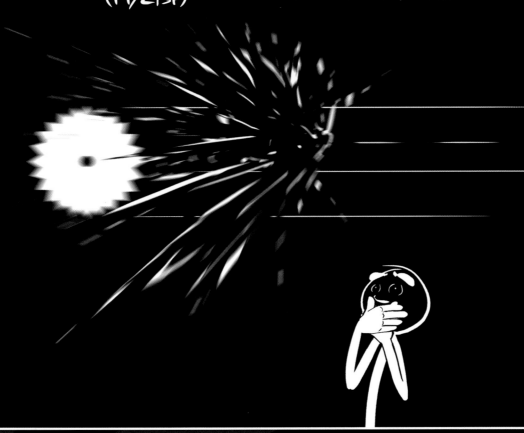

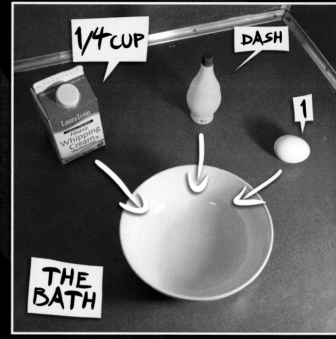

DREDGE

BREAD

FRY
IN OLIVE OIL
ON HIGH-
MEDIUM HEAT
UNTIL CRISPY

5-6
MINUTES

BAKE
25-30 MINS
@350F

ADD CHEESE TO
MELT AT END

MIX
THE SAUCE
SHOULD BE
ABOUT 3/4
CRANBERRY
TO 1/4
MAYO

SOME ASSEMBLY REQUIRED

EAT

Full Shopping List

CHICKEN BREAST (2)
EGG (1)
BREADCRUMBS (1/2c)
LEMON JUICE (DASH)
PECANS (1/4c)
CAYENNE (1tsp)
OREGANO (1tsp)
PAPRIKA (DASH)
HEAVY CREAM (1/4c)
MAYO
CRANBERRY SAUCE
TOMATO
LETTUCE
CHEESE

Notes

- A GOOD BUN CAN MAKE ALL THE DIFFERENCE. MINE WAS HOMEMADE. SEE PAGE 108.

- BE SURE YOUR PECANS ARE CRUSHED INTO PRETTY SMALL PIECES. BIGGER CHUNKS WON'T STICK.

- I LIKE TO MAKE A BIG BATCH OF THE CRANBERRY MAYO AND SAVE IT.

LASAGNA 101

DIFFICULTY

LIKE SUNDAY MORNING

SERVES: 6

SCORE SOME GROCERIES

RICOTTA CHEESE, COTTAGE CHEESE, MOZZARELLA, EGGS, LASAGNA NOODLES, MARINARA SAUCE AND PARMESAN

15oz RICOTTA

16oz COTTAGE

1/4c PARM

8oz MOZZ

2

ADD

GIVE IT A GOOD MIX

BEGIN CONSTRUCTION WITH A NOODLE LAYER

SPLIT-LEVEL CONSTRUCTION DIAGRAM

FOR SCIENCE

STACK AS HIGH AS YOU CAN, BUT ALWAYS END WITH A CHEESE LAYER

1/4c PARMESAN

SPRINKLE THE TOP WITH PARMESAN AND EXTRA MOZZARELLA

COVER

COOK @350F FOR 45 MINUTES

UNCOVER AND COOK ANOTHER 15 MINUTES

TIME TO KILL?

JUST SURVIVE

ENJOY

Full Shopping List

LASAGNA NOODLES (1 PACK)

MARINARA (~26oz)

COTTAGE CHEESE (16oz)

RICOTTA CHEESE (15oz)

MOZZARELLA (~8oz)

PARMESAN (1/2c)

EGGS (2)

Notes

- HOMEMADE MARINARA IS BEST. SEE PAGE 83.

- THIS IS ABOUT AS BASIC AS LASAGNA CAN GET. GO NUTS WITH IT.

- DO **NOT** PRECOOK YOUR LASAGNA NOODLES. THEY WILL COOK JUST FINE WHEN THE WHOLE THING IS BAKED.

- IN CASE THE CONSTRUCTION INSTRUCTION WASN'T CLEAR THE LAYERS WERE AS FOLLOWS: NOODLES, SAUCE, NOODLES, CHEESE, NOODLES, SAUCE, NOODLES, CHEESE, ETC. END ON A CHEESE LAYER.

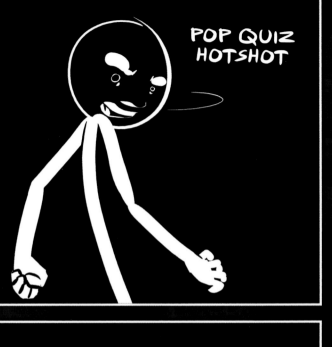

CHICKEN PARMESAN

FOR THE SEX

DIFFICULTY

PROPER DINNER
REQUIRES
PROPER EFFORT

SERVES: 4

ACT LIKE YOU'RE ABOUT TO COOK SOMETHING

CHICKN BREAST, OLIVE OIL, PARMESAN, ITALIAN BREADCRUMBS, NOODLES, HEAVY CREAM, MARINARA SAUCE, EGG

AIN'T NO MARINARA LIKE A HOMEMADE MARINARA 'CAUSE A HOMEMADE MARINARA DON'T STOP

SEE PAGE 83 JUST LEAVE OUT THE BEEF

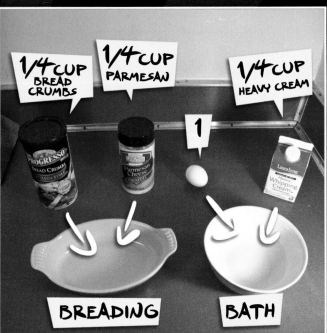

1/4 CUP BREAD CRUMBS

1/4 CUP PARMESAN

1/4 CUP HEAVY CREAM

1

BREADING

BATH

STOVE LOOKS LIKE THIS? PREHEAT OVEN TO 350F AND BEGIN NOODLES

OLIVE OIL IN PAN SET TO HIGH-MEDIUM HEAT

133

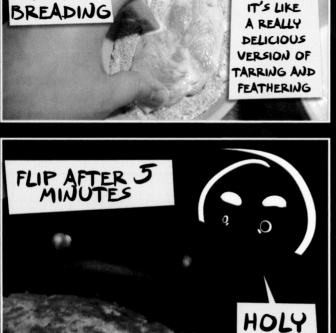

Full Shopping List

CHICKEN BREAST (2)
OLIVE OIL (~2 TBSP)
PARMESAN (1/4 C)
ITALIAN BREADCRUMBS (1/4 C)
NOODLES
HEAVY CREAM (1/4 C)
MARINARA SAUCE (26oz)
EGG (1)

Notes

- THIS RECIPE IS ESPECIALLY GREAT BECAUSE IT SEEMS WAY MORE COMPLICATED THAN IT ACTUALLY IS.

- YOU'LL HAVE PLENTY OF EGG MIXTURE LEFT SO IF YOU HAVE MORE THAN 2 CHICKEN BREASTS FEEL FREE TO FRY THEM UP WHILE YOU'RE AT IT.

- SERIOUSLY. LOOK UP THE DATES. WE WENT FROM NOT FLYING TO THE MOON IN THE SPAN OF A PERSON'S LIFETIME. NOW THINK ABOUT THE CRAZY SHIT YOU'LL SEE WHEN *YOU'RE* OLD.

OR YA KNOW WHATEVER. I'M SURE RAMEN NOODLES WILL BE IMPRESSIVE TOO.

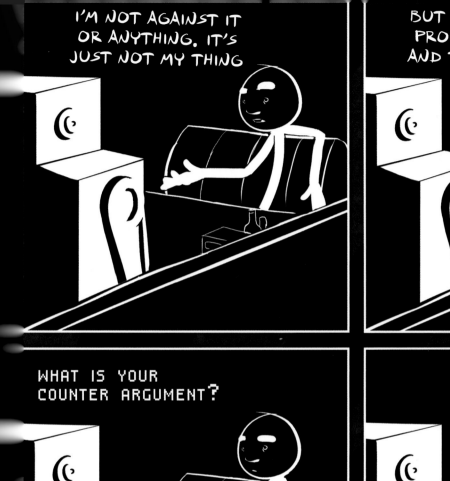

THE Vegan ONE

DIFFICULTY

IT'S "BOILING WATER" HARD

SERVES: 4

ARRANGE SPOILS FROM LOCAL SUPERMARCHÉ

NOODLES, OLIVE OIL, RED PEPPER, TOMATO, GARLIC, BASIL, SPINACH, LEMON JUICE, SALT AND PEPPER

BOIL NOODLES

ABOUT HALF THE BOX

DICE

3/4 CUP

1 CUP

2 CLOVES

ADD

2 TBSP BASIL

1 CUP SPINACH

ADD A DRIZZLE OF OLIVE OIL AND TOSS

STRAIN AND ADD PASTA

ADD A DRIZZLE OF OLIVE OIL AND TOSS

NOW WITH 100% MORE NOODLE

ADD ALL OF THIS TO TASTE

DEMAND TO SEE LIFE'S MANAGER

ENJOY YOUR UTTERLY HEALTHFUL, MEAT-FREE AND LET'S NOT FORGET, DELICIOUS DINNER

Full Shopping list

NOODLES (~1/2 BOX)
OLIVE OIL (DRIZZLE)
RED PEPPER (3/4C)
TOMATO (1C)
GARLIC (2 CLOVES)
BASIL (2 TBSP)
SPINACH (1C)
LEMON JUICE
SALT AND PEPPER

Notes

-IF YOU CAN GET ALL FRESH INGREDIENTS, USE ALL FRESH INGREDIENTS.

-BABY SPINACH IS RECOMMENDED.

-I'LL BE HONEST, I WAS SURPRISED AT JUST HOW GOOD THIS WAS. I'LL BET YOU'LL BE TOO.

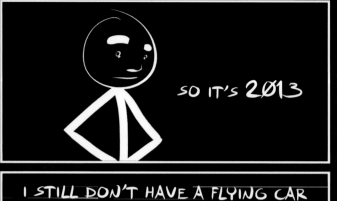

SO IT'S 2013

I STILL DON'T HAVE A FLYING CAR

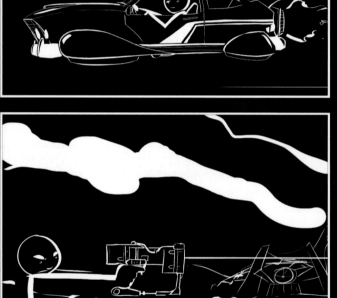

OR A SWEET LASER GUN

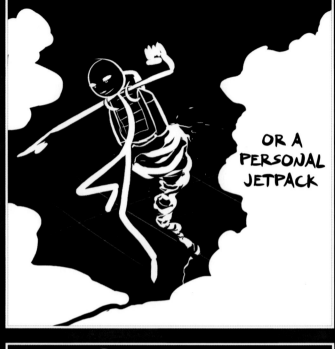

OR A PERSONAL JETPACK

BUT YOU'VE GOTTA BE GRATEFUL FOR WHAT YOU DO HAVE

LIKE SWEET DELICIOUS BEEF

MEATLOAF 2013

DIFFICULTY

YOU'LL GET A LITTLE DIRTY

SERVES: 4

143

BRING OUT YOUR GROCERIES

FOR THE GLAZE

BEEF, RED PEPPER, ONION, GARLIC, EGGS, BREADCRUMBS, SALT AND PEPPER, CAYENNE, CHILI POWDER, SAGE, MILK, KETCHUP, WORCESTERSHIRE SAUCE, HONEY, CUMIN, MUSTARD, BROWN SUGAR

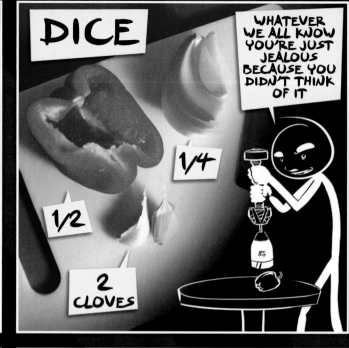

DICE

WHATEVER WE ALL KNOW YOU'RE JUST JEALOUS BECAUSE YOU DIDN'T THINK OF IT

1/4

1/2

2 CLOVES

ADD

2/3c

1 TSP CHILI POWDER

DASH PEPPER

3/4c MILK

DASH SALT

DASH SAGE

2

DASH CAYENNE

GET MESSY

144

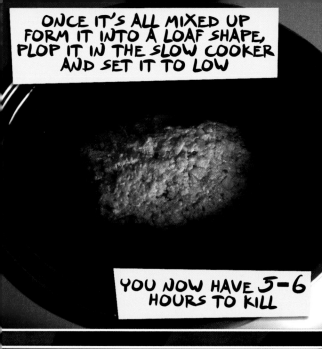

ONCE IT'S ALL MIXED UP FORM IT INTO A LOAF SHAPE, PLOP IT IN THE SLOW COOKER AND SET IT TO LOW

YOU NOW HAVE 5-6 HOURS TO KILL

GO DO SOME LIVING

AND DON'T FORGET TO MIX UP THAT GLAZE

1/2 TSP CUMIN

DASH MUSTARD AND WORCESTER

1 TBSP HONEY

DASH B.SUGAR

MIX

1/2 C KETCHUP

ABOUT 30 MINUTES BEFORE TIME IS UP APPLY THE GLAZE AND CONTINUE COOKING UNTIL DONE

SLICE

AND CONSUME

Full Shopping List

GROUND BEEF (1 1/2LB)
EGGS (2)
ONION (1/4)
GARLIC (2 CLOVES)
RED BELL PEPPER (1/2)
MILK (3/4C)
SALT (DASH)
PEPPER (DASH)
CHILI POWDER (1TSP)
SAGE (DASH)
BREAD CRUMBS (2/3C)
CAYENNE (DASH)
WORCESTERSHIRE (DASH)
DIJON MUSTARD (DASH)
HONEY (1TBSP)
BROWN SUGAR (DASH)
CUMIN (1/2TSP)
KETCHUP (1/2C)

Notes

- WHEN MIXING EVERYTHING IN WITH THE BEEF THE CONSISTENCY SHOULD BE JUST ENOUGH TO HOLD TOGETHER. ADJUST WITH ADDITIONAL BREADCRUMBS (IF TOO WET) OR MILK (IF TOO DRY) TO GET IT RIGHT.

- IF I KEEP DOING THIS LONG ENOUGH EVENTUALLY I'LL HAVE A RECIPE CALLED MEAT LOAF 2033. TALK ABOUT PLAYING THE LONG GAME...

147

THE GREATEST TACO IN THE WORLD

(TRIBUTE)

DIFFICULTY

EASY AS CASTING OUT LOW-LEVEL HELLSPAWN

SERVES: 4

I GATHERED THE FIRST INGREDIENTS THAT CAME TO MY HEAD

BEEF, TORTILLA, TOMATO, RED PEPPER, ONION, CHEDDAR, LETTUCE, CAYENNE, PAPRIKA, SALT, PEPPER, CUMIN, ONION POWDER, GARLIC POWDER, CHIPOTLE POWDER, CHILI POWDER

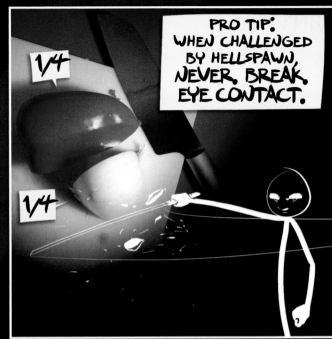

1/4

1/4

PRO TIP: WHEN CHALLENGED BY HELLSPAWN, NEVER, BREAK, EYE CONTACT.

SAUTÉ

BROWN

THE SECRET TO THE BEST SEASONING IN THE WORLD IS NOT GIVING A DAMN

EYEBALL ALL THE THINGS

OR CHECK THE NOTES P. 153

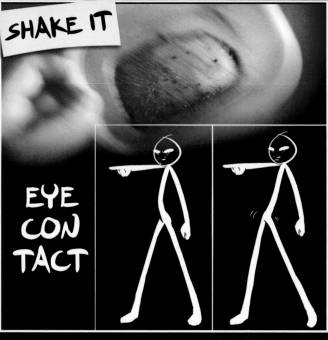

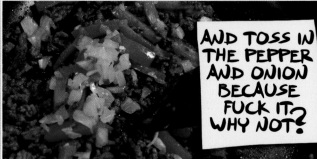

I ASSEMBLED MY MASTERPIECE

IN ALL ITS GLORY

NEEDLESS TO SAY...

THE BEAST WAS STUNNED.

Full Shopping list

CHILI POWDER (1TBSP)
CAYENNE (DASH)
PAPRIKA (DASH)
SALT (DASH)
PEPPER (DASH)
CUMIN (DASH)
ONION POWDER (DASH)
GARLIC POWDER (DASH)
CHIPOTLE POWDER (DASH)
BEEF (1/2 LB)
RED PEPPER (1/4)
ONION (1/4)
CHEDDAR
LETTUCE
TORTILLAS
TOMATO

Notes

- THESE ARE NOT THE GREATEST TACOS IN THE WORLD. THESE ARE JUST A TRIBUTE.

- FOR THE SEASONING START WITH A TBSP OF CHILI POWDER AND A DASH OF EVERYTHING ELSE. IT'S DIFFERENT EVERY TIME I MAKE IT AND THAT'S HOW IT SHOULD BE.

- "WHY ANGUS?" 1. MACGYVER. 2. AC/DC. 3. BEEF.

DESSERTS

THE BANANARAMA

A TASTY FROZEN TREAT FOR THOSE "CRUEL SUMMERS"

DIFFICULTY

IF YOUR BARRIER OF ENTRY TO COOKING IS A BLENDER... WE NEED TO TALK

SERVES: 4

BUT YOU WON'T

ISOLATE SOME PIECES OF REESE'S IN A BAG

IF YOU CAN DO THIS WITHOUT EATING ONE THE EARTH WILL EXPLODE

AND TRUST ME, YOU DON'T WANT TO BE THAT GUY

SMASH 'EM UP

PUT YOUR REESE'S PIECES PIECES TO THE SIDE

GO ABOUT YOUR DAY

FOR 3Ø MINUTES OR SO

LATER

IT BLENDS

FOR A MINUTE

THEN YOU'LL NEED TO USE A SPOON TO SCRAPE IT OFF THE SIDES AND KEEP BLENDING

BUT BEFORE YOU KNOW IT...

DAMN, SON!

THAT'S CALRISSIAN SMOOTH

PB — 1 SCOOP

ICECREAM — 2 SCOOPS

PIECES!

BLEND!

BOWL IT

TO THE FREEZER TO FIRM UP

~1 HOUR

I WANT MY FATHER BACK YOU SON OF A BITCH!

Note: **ENJOY THAT BANANA-LACED GOODNESS**

Full Shopping list

BANANAS (~3)

ICE CREAM
(2 scoops)

PEANUT BUTTER
(1 scoop)

REESE'S PIECES
(UP TO YOU)

Notes

- If you leave it in the freezer too long it will firm up too much. You should be ready to eat it after the initial cooling. Otherwise you'll need to thaw it just a bit before eating again.

- Inigo... right in the feels. Every time.

DAMN DIRTY APE BREAD

BREAD

DIFFICULTY

AS EASY AS IT IS
TASTY (VERY)

SERVES: 4

REQUIRED ITEMS

CANNED BISCUITS, RAISINS (OPTIONAL), SUGAR, CINNAMON, BROWN SUGAR, BUTTER AND A BUNT PAN

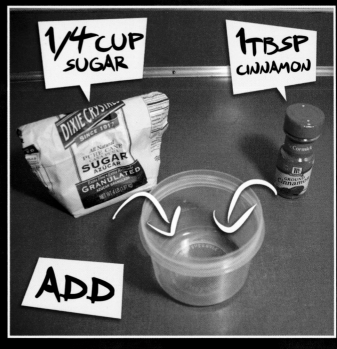

1/4 CUP SUGAR

1 TBSP CINNAMON

ADD

SHAKE IT

BISCUIT EVOLUTION

BISCUITS QUARTERED, ROLLED INTO BALLS AND COATED IN THE SUGAR/CINNAMON MIX BEFORE GOING IN THE PAN

163

ENJOY

Full Shopping List

BISCUITS
(2 16oz CANS)
RAISINS (OPTIONAL)
SUGAR (1/4 c)
CINNAMON (1TBSP)
BROWN SUGAR (1/2 c)
BUTTER (6TBSP)
A BUNDT PAN

Notes

- PECANS ARE ALSO A GOOD ADDITION.

- THESE ARE ABSURDLY GOOD FOR THE EFFORT THAT GOES INTO THEM AND ARE SUPER EASY TO EAT. GREAT FOR GET-TOGETHERS.

- WHEN COATING THE BISCUITS IN THE CINNAMON/SUGAR THE CINNAMON GOES FASTER SO YOU SHOULD OCCASIONALY REPLENISH IT AS YOU GO TO KEEP THE CONSISTENCY THE SAME THROUGHOUT.

PUMPKIN BUTTERSCOTCH COOKIES

DIFFICULTY

YOU'LL HAVE TO BEAT BACK ONLOOKERS

SERVES: 4

GRAB THIS STUFF NEXT TIME YOU'RE OUT

FLOUR, BROWN SUGAR, EGG, VANILLA, BAKING POWDER, BAKING SODA, VEG OIL, PUMPKIN PUREE, CINNAMON, CLOVES, ALLSPICE

1/2 TSP BAKING SODA, BAKING POWDER, AND CINNAMON

DASH CLOVES

1/8 TSP ALLSPICE

1/4 TSP SALT

1 CUP FLOUR

ADD

WHISK TOGETHER TO REMOVE LUMPS

OH SO SMOOTH

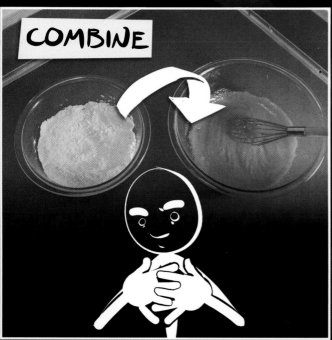

SCOOP ON TO PAN AND BAKE

15-18 MINUTES @325F

FIN

FULL SHOPPING LIST

FLOUR (1C)
BROWN SUGAR (1/2C)
EGG (1)
VANILLA (1/2 TSP)
BAKING POWDER (1/2 TSP)
BAKING SODA (1/2 TSP)
VEG OIL (1/4 C)
PUMPKIN PUREE (1/2 C)
CINNAMON (1/2 TSP)
CLOVES (DASH)
ALLSPICE (1/8 TSP)

NOTES

- THE COOKIES COME OUT VERY CAKELIKE, BUT I FOUND THIS TO BE A VERY HAPPY ACCIDENT.

- DON'T LIKE BUTTERSCOTCH? GIVE NUTELLA A TRY INSTEAD.

- PLAY IT AGAIN, SAM.

WHIPPERSNAP

HOMEMADE,
BOURBON-WFUSED
WHIP CREAM

DIFFICULTY

MY CAT COULD
MAKE THIS.
AND I DON'T
HAVE A CAT

1 TBSP

GATHER AND MIX

1 TBSP

1 CUP

WHISK LIKE YOUR LIFE DEPENDS ON IT

OR JUST PRETEND YOU'RE PLAYING WII

FIRESTARTER METHOD (ACTUALLY WORKS)

Be Rough With It.

THE IDEA IS TO FILL IT WITH AIR TO MAKE IT FLUFF. IT WILL TAKE A LITTLE WHILE BUT ONCE IT STARTS TO THICKEN, IT WILL THICKEN QUICK. YOU'LL KNOW WHEN IT IS THE RIGHT CONSISTENCY. STOP THERE.

BECAUSE YOU'RE DONE

Full Shopping List

HEAVY WHIPPING
CREAM (1CUP)

POWDERED SUGAR
(1TBSP)

YOUR CHOICE OF
BOURBON (1TBSP)

A WHISK

Notes

- OBVIOUSLY YOU DON'T HAVE TO USE
BOURBON. YOU CAN ADD MOST ANYTHING
YOU WANT TO DIRECT THE FLAVOR IN
WHATEVER DIRECTION YOU LIKE (JUST
DON'T ADD SO MUCH THAT IT DOESN'T
WHIP). THE BOURBON JUST HAPPENS TO
GO EXTREMELY WELL WITH THE PANCAKES
I'M MAKING NEXT, AMONG OTHER THINGS.

- BE PATIENT, IT WILL TAKE A FEW
MINUTES OF WHISKING. AND DO NOT
OVER WHIP, IT WILL BECOME LUMPY AND
RUNNY AGAIN. STOP AT COOL WHIP
CONSISTENCY.

STRAWBERRY DIABEETUS ICE CREAM

DIFFICULTY

IT'S ONLY THAT HIGH BECAUSE IT'S SO DAMN HARD TO WAIT FOR

SERVES: 4

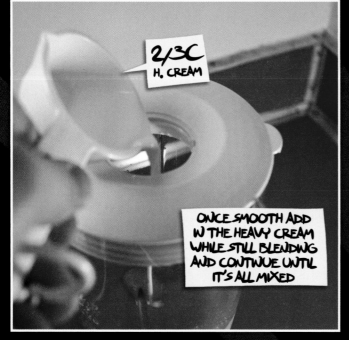

Full Shopping List

FROZEN
STRAWBERRIES
(10oz)

HEAVY CREAM
(2/3c)

SUGAR
(1/2c)

Notes

- Any frozen fruit (or combination of fruits) will work. Not just strawberries.

- This does really turn out pretty rich. You probably won't be able to eat too much at a time.

- You can leave it in the freezer as long as you like. It will be scoopable even when fully frozen.

- Fuck that blender. Seriously.

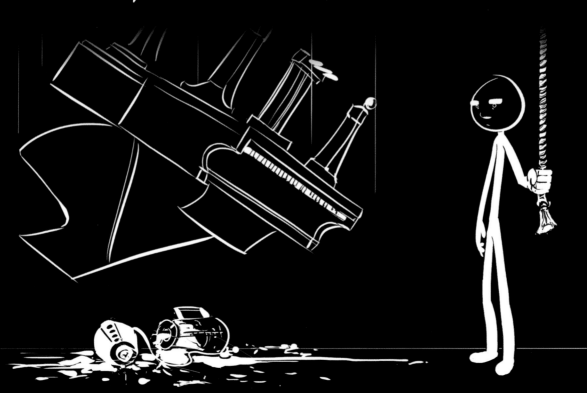

CHEESECAKE of CHAMPIONS

DIFFICULTY

PIECE OF CAKE (NO LIE)

SERVES: 6

ACCRUE FOODS

CREAM CHEESE, EGGS, PUMPKIN PUREE, VANILLA, CLOVES, CINNAMON, NUTMEG, SUGAR, NUTELLA

2 PACKS CREAM CHEESE

1/2 CUP SUGAR

1/2 TSP VANILLA

2

ONCE SMOOTH SPREAD THIN LAYER W THE PIE CRUST

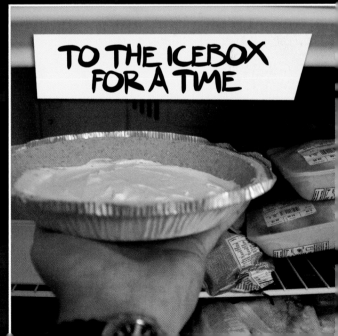

TO THE ICEBOX FOR A TIME

FULL SHOPPING LIST

PUREED PUMPKIN (1/2c)
CREAM CHEESE (2 8oz PACKS)
EGGS (2)
PIE CRUST (1)
NUTELLA (1/3c)
GROUND NUTMEG (DASH)
GROUND CLOVES (DASH)
CINNAMON (1/2 TSP)
SUGAR (1/2c)
VANILLA EXTRACT (1/2 TSP)

NOTES

- BUYING ALL OF THE SPICES SEPARATELY CAN BE EXPENSIVE. ESPECIALY THE CLOVES. SINCE YOU ONLY NEED A PINCH OF CLOVES YOU CAN EASILY FORGO THEM AND LOOK FOR SOMETHING CALLED "APPLE PIE SPICE" WHICH HAS CINNAMON, NUTMEG, AND ALLSPICE ALL IN ONE. IT SHOULD WORK JUST FINE.

- SERIOUSLY. HAND-MIXERS. USEFUL.

Recipe Index

Appetizers and Sides   1

Jalapeño Poppers 2

Dem Wedges 7

Cheese in a Snuggie 12

The Artichoke Dip 17

Corny Bread 21

Cheddar Boss Biscuits 26

Steezy Mac 31

Mash Tatoes 35

Breakfast   40

Sexy Pancakes 41

The MacGuffin Muffin 47

Maple Bacon 53

The Perfect Scrambled Egg 56

Oatmeal Pancakes 62

Bacon, Egg & Cheese 66

Lunch and Dinner 70

Pulled Pork 71
Super Teriyaki Burger 78
Bolognese for Days 83
That's My JAMbalaya 87
The Chickeniest Chicken Soup 91
2am Chili 96
Deep Dish Pizza 103
Fucking Bread Bowls 108
The Classic (burger) 116
The Chicken Sandwich 122
Lasagna 101 127
Chicken Parmesan 131
The Vegan One 137
Meatloaf 2013 142
The Greatest Taco
in the World (Tribute) 147

Desserts 154

The Bananarama 155
Damn Dirty Ape Bread 161
Pumpkin Butterscotch Cookies 165
Whippersnap 170
Strawberry Diabeetus Ice cream 174
Cheesecake of Champions 178

Metric Conversions

TSP — ML		TBSP — ML		CUP — ML		°F — °C		OZ — G		LBS — KG	
1/8	.5	1/4	3.5	1/4	59	325	163	5	142	1	.5
1/4	1	1/2	7.5	1/3	79	350	177	8	228	1.5	.7
1/2	2.5	1	14.5	1/2	118	375	190	10	283	3.5	1.6
1	5			1	236	400	204	16	453	7	3.2
						425	218	28	794		
						450	232				

THANKS FOR READING